T0345969

CAMBRIDGE
UNIVERSITY PRESS

University Printing House, Cambridge CB2 8BS, United Kingdom

Cambridge University Press is part of the University of Cambridge.

It furthers the University's mission by disseminating knowledge in the pursuit of education, learning and research at the highest international levels of excellence.

www.cambridge.org
Information on this title: www.cambridge.org/9781107492295

© Cambridge University Press 1952

First published 1952
Re-issued 2015

A catalogue record for this publication is available from the British Library

ISBN 978-1-107-49229-5 Paperback

THE ATHENS OF
DEMOSTHENES

BY

A. H. M. JONES

Demosthenes' aims and policy have often been
discussed, but his biographers have rarely paid
much attention to the Athenians to whom he spoke.
We are left with the general impression that, in
contrast with the patriotic orator, they were an
idle, cowardly, pleasure-loving crew, who would
not fight or pay their taxes, but preferred to draw
their dole at home, paying—or rather failing to
pay—mercenaries to fight their battles. Is this
estimate just? It is the picture which appears to
emerge from Demosthenes' speeches, which, with
those of contemporary orators, afford almost all
the evidence available. This evidence I propose to
examine afresh.

'Pay war tax' (εἰσφέρετε), and 'serve yourselves
in the army' (αὐτοὶ στρατεύεσθε) are the two key-
notes of Demosthenes' appeals to the people. Let
us first examine the war tax. It is a highly technical
and controversial subject, and I hope that you will
excuse me if I am somewhat dogmatic. The

questions which I wish to answer are: Was it, as is generally believed, a progressive tax? How many people paid it, and what was the limit of exemption? How much money was actually raised?

The εἰσφορά was a war tax, raised by decree of the people as occasion demanded, and took the form of a capital levy. For this purpose a census of property was held in 378/7 B.C., in which according to Polybius 'the total assessment' (τὸ σύμπαν τίμημα) of Attica was valued at 5750 talents;[1] Demosthenes speaks of 'the assessment of the country' (τὸ τίμημα...τῆς χώρας) as being in his day 6000 talents, and reckons levies as percentages of this sum—1 per cent will bring in 60 talents, 2 per cent 120 talents and so forth.[2] Now Polybius clearly thought that the τίμημα represented the total capital (land, houses and other property) of the country—he ignores the fact that it excludes properties below the exemption limit—and represented its real value. Demosthenes, however, in one passage of his first speech against Aphobus[3] uses τίμημα in another sense: 'three talents is the assessment of fifteen talents', he says (πεντεκαίδεκα ταλάντων γὰρ τρία τάλαντα τίμημα), and he implies that for smaller fortunes the proportion was less than one-fifth. On this passage, together with an obscure citation in Pollux,[4] has been built the theory that the τίμημα was not the real value of a man's

2

property, but the taxable value, and that the taxable value was a higher proportion of the real value for the rich than for the poor, so that the εἰσφορά was the only known progressive tax of antiquity.

This theory involves very serious difficulties. In the first place it seems very perverse that even the richest should be assessed at one-fifth of their capital; the natural course would have been to assess them at the whole, and scale down the assessment of the poorer classes only. In the second place the theory conflicts with a contemporary inscription,[5] a lease in which the tenant is to pay 54 drachmae a year rent and the εἰσφοραί, if any, κατὰ τὸ τίμημα καθ᾽ ἑπτὰ μνᾶς; the rent works out at about 8 per cent if 7 minae is the real value of the property, but is absurd if the real value is five or more times that sum. It also makes the total τίμημα of Attica absurd. 6000 talents is perhaps rather a low sum, but it excludes, we must remember, thousands of small properties below the exemption limit, and, as frequent allusions in the orators show,[6] concealment of wealth and under-assessment was the rule rather than the exception. On the other hand it is quite impossible that the value of Athenian property assessable for tax can have been not merely five times 6000 talents, but much more. Τίμημα is then used in two senses—to denote the real value in the inscription and in the phrase τὸ τίμημα τῆς χώρας; and as Demosthenes uses it in the first speech against Aphobus. And moreover εἰσφορά was levied on τίμημα in the first sense of real value, or Demosthenes' calculation that a 1 per cent levy will yield 60 talents is nonsense. Demosthenes must be using the word in an untechnical way in the passage in which he states that the τίμημα of 15 talents is 3 talents for the largest fortunes.

Now Demosthenes alludes several times to this 1:5 ratio, but in all the other passages[7] he uses different phraseology: ταύτην ἠξίουν εἰσφέρειν τὴν εἰσφοράν, he says, or κατὰ τὰς πέντε καὶ εἴκοσι μνᾶς πεντακοσίας δραχμὰς εἰσφέρειν, as if his guardians put him down to pay one-fifth of his fortune as tax. Of course tax was never levied at this fantastic rate—actually during the ten years of his minority Demosthenes paid 18 minae on the 15 talents at which he was assessed.[8] What do Demosthenes' phrases mean? Mr Meiggs[9] has recently suggested that the one-fifth is a ceiling, the highest sum which the richest class could be asked to pay as the total of all their tax payments during their lifetime; for the poorer categories of taxpayers this ceiling would be lower. Εἰσφορά was then levied as a given percentage of the real value of all taxable properties, and was not a progressive tax: but if successive levies came to a total of say a twentieth (the actual figures are unknown) of their capital, men of the

4

poorest class could claim exemption, while men of the richest class would go on paying till a fifth of their capital was exhausted.

The theory is attractive in that it gives a meaning to Demosthenes' phraseology and tallies with Greek ways of thinking: they tended to regard a man's fortune as a static sum, ignoring income, and to set off against it the total of his payments on trierarchies, liturgies and εἰσφοραί.[10] But to put such a system into practice would have involved calculations of great complexity; for in fact fortunes were not static, but rose and fell by inheritances and investment of surplus income on the one hand, and payment of dowries and sales of assets on the other. I find it hard to believe that so complicated a system could have worked and I submit an alternative explanation of Demosthenes' words, which was suggested to me by my former pupil, Mr de Ste Croix. In one passage Demosthenes states that his guardians made him president (ἡγεμών) of his symmory not on a small valuation but on so high a one as to pay 500 drachmae on 25 minae.[11] Now the ἡγεμόνες with the δεύτεροι and τρίτοι of the symmories later constituted the 300 προεισφέροντες,[12] who advanced the tax to the state, subsequently recovering it from the other members of their symmories. May it not be that this system existed from the beginning of the symmories, and that it was liability for the προεισφορά which was scaled up to one-fifth of the payer's fortune according to his wealth?

There are difficulties in this view also. There were in 357 arrears amounting to about 14 talents on the 300 odd talents which had been demanded in the previous twenty years.[13] Some of these arrears may have been due from members of the 300; it is perhaps significant that of the individual debtors mentioned by Demosthenes two are known to have been trierarchs,[14] and must therefore have been fairly wealthy men, who might have been enrolled in the 300. But at any rate half of the total arrears was made up out of quite small sums, scarcely any according to Demosthenes over 1 mina;[15] which implies 400 or 500 debtors. How did all these taxpayers still owe money to the treasury if their tax had been advanced by the 300? They might still owe money to members of the 300, but not to the State.

Two answers are possible. It may be that the προεισφορά was a device designed for use in emergencies only, and was rarely or not at all employed in the twenty years in question. Or again the original function of the 300 may have been not to prepay but to guarantee or underwrite the tax of their symmories; this is perhaps suggested by the use of εἰσφέρειν and not προεισφέρειν in connexion with the 300 in the earliest reference to them.[16] In that case the guarantee may well never have been enforced, for there was little enthusiasm to collect the tax when once the emergency which had demanded it was past.[17]

The second difficulty is that when in 362 an emergency levy was raised to finance a naval expedition, the people decreed that the members of the council should nominate on behalf of their demes persons who were members of the deme or owned land in it to advance the levy to the State.[18] Here the 300 are entirely ignored, and it has generally been assumed that they did not yet exist. It was, on the usual view, the emergency of 362 which first called for a προεισφορά and the procedure described above was a first experiment, which led to the establishment of a standing body of 300 προ-εισφέροντες.

One objection to this view is that in a speech delivered a few years before, Isaeus[19] alludes to the 300 as an established institution connected with the εἰσφορά. A second is that about 376 (that is directly after the establishment of the symmory system) Demosthenes was made ἡγεμών of his symmory, though a child of seven, because of his wealth: the post of ἡγεμών, that is, was not executive but carried financial responsibility from the first. It seems a necessary inference that the 300 comprising

the ἡγεμόνες, δεύτεροι and τρίτοι of the 100 symmories were from the beginning financially responsible for the tax due from their groups, either by
prepaying or by underwriting it. Indeed this would
seem to be the whole point of the symmory system.

It was not then because the 300 did not yet exist
that the people in 362 decreed that προεισφέροντες
be nominated *ad hoc* in each deme. It may be that
a προεισφορά had been levied very recently, and that
the 300 had claimed that their hands were already
full; if there had been a levy in the previous year
they could, since the προεισφορά was a liturgy, have
legally claimed exemption.[20] Or alternatively it
may be that the symmory system through long
disuse had become so disorganized that when
a sudden emergency arose it had to be abandoned
and *ad hoc* measures adopted. In favour of this
view it may be noted that the emergency legislation
ignores not only the 300, but, it would seem, the
whole symmory system: for it is implied that the
collection was made not by symmories but by
demes.[21] It may even be that this levy was not
a normal εἰσφορά, but a special tax on some other
basis, substituted for it either because the capacity
of the war taxpayers was temporarily exhausted or
because the machinery for assessing and collecting
a war tax was seriously out of gear. The speaker
uses the words προεισφέρειν and προεισφορά, but these

may not be technical terms but mean merely 'to prepay a levy'. On the other hand he alludes to the magistrates who were in charge of the levy as οἱ τὰ στρατιωτικὰ εἰσπράττοντες,[22] which suggests a special military levy rather than a regular εἰσφορά.

The object of this long argument has been to prove that the εἰσφορά was not a progressive tax, that is, that all liable to it paid the same proportion of their capital, whether they were rich or poor. Now for my second question, How many citizens paid? That the number was large is implied by Demosthenes' language in several passages; he speaks for instance of the mass of the people (τῷ πλήθει τῷ ὑμετέρῳ) as being exhausted by payment of war tax.[23] A rather more precise answer is, I think, possible. There were, it is generally agreed, 100 war tax symmories as against 20 trierarchic symmories.[24] The 20 trierarchic symmories, which were modelled on those of the εἰσφορά, comprised 1200 persons, at 60 per symmory.[25] The 100 war tax symmories on the same basis will have included 6000 persons. What was the exemption limit? Demosthenes several times alludes to 25 minae as a basic assessment unit— κατὰ τὰς πέντε καὶ εἴκοσι μνᾶς πεντακοσίας δραχμὰς εἰσφέρειν[26]—and, on one occasion, even more significantly assumes it as such—πέντε μνᾶς συνετάξατ' εἰσφέρειν, meaning to pay one-fifth.[27] This suggests that 25 minae was the minimum taxable capital.

This would accord with what other figures we have. In 322 B.C. Antipater, limiting the franchise to citizens owning over 2000 drachmae (or 20 minae), found that there were 9000 who qualified.[28] If there were 9000 persons who owned more than 20 minae each, there might well be about 6000 who owned more than 25 minae.

Finally how much war tax was actually levied? In his speech against Androtion Demosthenes tells us that the levies between 377 and 357 totalled perhaps 300 talents or a little more;[29] this works out at 0·25 per cent per annum on the assessment of 6000 talents. Demosthenes during his ten years' minority (376–366) paid 18 minae on his assessment of 15 talents,[30] which works out at about 0·2 per cent per annum. This is on capital, of course, but reckoning income as 10 per cent of capital, which is about right taking land and money together, levies during this period, which was full of wars, represented only a 2 to $2\frac{1}{2}$ per cent income tax, or in modern terms 5d. to 6d. in the pound. We may therefore with some justification be amused when Xenophon speaks of the Athenians during this very time as 'worn out by levies of war tax' (ἀποκναιόμενοι χρημάτων εἰσφοραῖς).[31] But taxation is a matter of habit—our great-grandfathers were outraged by an extra penny in the pound—and the Athenians never could form the habit of paying war tax since it was an occasional payment and, when it came, relatively heavy—Demosthenes speaks of 1 per cent and even 2 per cent as normal,[32] and these are equivalent to an income tax of 2*s*. and 4*s*. in the pound. And before we blame the Athenians too loudly we should remember that there was no personal allowance, wife's allowance or children's allowance to soften the blow to the poor man with a large family. Demosthenes is probably justified in invoking the jurors' sympathy for 'the farmers who pinch and scrape, but owing to the cost of bringing up their children and domestic expenses and other public demands have fallen into arrears of war tax'.[33] It must have meant much pinching to bring up a family on a farm worth 25 minae. One litigant, indeed, states that 'my father left me and my brother property of only 45 minae each, and it is not easy to live on that'.[34] On the basis of the single fourth-century figure that we possess for the price of land,[35] a farm worth 25 minae would have comprised about 7 acres—without stock, implements, house or furniture. If let at the rate of 8 per cent, which seems to have been normal,[36] it would have brought in a rent of 200 drachmae a year; and bare food for a single man, without counting clothes, shoes or any extras, cost 180 drachmae.[37] The proprietor of such a holding normally of course worked it himself with the aid of his family, and would make a larger income than the rental value, but even so little enough to feed a family.

An ill-adjusted system of war tax meant then that while the rich got off relatively very lightly, the mass of poor taxpayers were really embarrassed by even an occasional small levy, and were very reluctant to vote one. Actually very little was raised. How then did Athens pay for her wars? For the answer one may turn to Isocrates' panegyric on Timotheus.[38] Timotheus' great merit, it appears, was that he was a very cheap general. He received only 13 talents from the treasury for his great campaign round the Peloponnese in which he won Corcyra in 375. Apollodorus gives a vivid picture of his financial straits two years later, when he had to mortgage his estates and borrow right and left to keep his sixty ships together,[39] and Iphicrates his successor had to hire out his rowers as agricultural labourers in the intervals between operations.[40] For the campaign which resulted in the capture of Samos in 365 Timotheus received no public funds, and he financed the capture of Potidaea and other Thrace-ward cities in the following year from the contributions of the local allies.

These facts affect Demosthenes' second slogan, hoplite service. The Athenians cannot be accused of cowardice. They turned out for campaigns in the good old fifth-century style in Boeotia, Euboea, the Peloponnese and even as far afield as Thessaly. In 369 they raised a levy *en masse* in support of Sparta against Thebes; 6000 fought at Mantinea in 362; 5000 foot and 400 horse at Thermopylae in 352. For Chaeronea there was a levy *en masse*, and 5000 foot and 500 horse fought in the Lamian war.[41] The Athenians did not object to fighting. What they were afraid of may be deduced from the scheme for a small standing army which Demosthenes put forward in the *First Philippic*. The Athenian element is to serve for a fixed period, not a long one at that, by a regular system of reliefs;[42] and the State, he insists, must make financial provision for paying them a ration allowance at the meagre rate of 2 obols a day[43]—by way of comparison ephebes (young men doing their military training in Attica) were allowed 4 obols a day for their food under Lycurgus' regime,[44] and even public slaves got 3 obols a day.[45] They will make up the balance, Demosthenes euphemistically hopes, ἀπὸ τοῦ πολέμου.

In two other passages Demosthenes implies that hoplites were normally expected to keep themselves. In the *de Falsa Legatione*[46] he estimates the cost of the expedition to Thermopylae at 200 talents, 'if you count the private expenditure of those who served', and in the *First Olynthiac*[47] he asserts that 'if you had to serve abroad yourselves for only thirty days, and take what you would need

13

on service from the produce of the country—while no enemy was in the country, I mean—those of you who are farmers would I think suffer a heavier loss than all you have spent on the war up to date'.

What the Athenian hoplite dreaded, then, was being shipped off to Macedonia and left there to starve for an indefinite period, while the farm or the business at home went to rack and ruin. Things were very different from the good old days of the fifth century, when a hoplite got 2 drachmae a day.[48] And it must be remembered that many hoplites were quite poor men; the qualification is generally, and probably correctly, believed to have been property to the value of 2000 drachmae[49]—roughly five acres and a cow. Demosthenes in the *Meidias* is quite apologetic for introducing to the jury a poor hoplite witness—πένης μὲν ἴσως ἐστίν, οὐ πονηρὸς δέ γε—a curious remark in a speech devoted to abuse of Meidias, ὁ πλούσιος.[50] Lysias' client Mantitheus, when his deme assembled for the muster, found that many of his poorer fellow hoplites could not raise their journey money and organized a subscription to supply each with 30 drachmae.[51]

The same considerations applied *a fortiori* to naval service, which Demosthenes also frequently urged on the citizens, since it was thetes who served in the fleet. It may be noted that at this period Athens could not rely on volunteers to row her triremes, but conscription was regularly employed.[52] If one reads Apollodorus' speech against Polycles one realizes why. Gone were the days of a drachma a day;[53] for two months only did the men get any pay, for the remaining year and five months only rations, and even the ration money was often short, and failed altogether for the return voyage.[54] For a man with a wife and family to keep this meant disaster, and it is little wonder if, as Apollodorus says, whenever a trireme put back to Athens in the middle of the year, large numbers deserted and the rest refused to sail again unless they were given something to provide for their families (εἰς διοίκησιν τῶν οἰκείων).[55]

Lack of public funds naturally increased the expenses of trierarchs also. In 373 Timotheus made his sixty trierarchs each advance 7 minae to feed their crews:[56] he being a rich man was able to cover this advance by mortgages on his estates, but other trierarchs were less fortunate; Apollodorus had to borrow freely from his father's correspondents overseas.[57] The main vice of the trierarchy, however, was the faulty working of the symmory system. Trierarchic symmories were introduced in 357 B.C.[58] because the trierarchy or syntrierarchy, whereby one or two men were responsible for the upkeep of a trireme for one year, was found too heavy a burden on some of the persons liable. But no rules seem to have been laid down for sharing the expenses within the symmory and the general practice was that all members paid an equal share. This resulted, as Demosthenes explains in the *Meidias* and the *de Corona*, in the richest members, who could well afford to be sole trierarchs two or three times over, paying one-sixteenth of a trierarchy, while the same amount was paid by the poorer members of the 1200 who could ill afford it.[59] Demosthenes' first scheme of reform, set out in the speech on the symmories, was ill conceived; he proposed, it is true, to make payments proportional to property, but he also suggested spreading the burden yet wider over the whole body of war tax-payers.[60] The result would have been to make the trierarchy a supplementary war tax, with all its unfairness. Later Demosthenes grasped the real point, and threw the whole burden of the trierarchy on the 300 richest citizens in proportion to their means, so that some performed two trierarchies.[61]

You have no doubt been long waiting for me to mention the θεωρικόν, which occupies a larger space in Demosthenes' commentators than in his speeches, and was of greater political than financial importance—as Demosthenes himself says, 'The sum of money about which you are debating is small, but the habit of mind which goes with it is important'.[62] The fund consisted of τὰ περιόντα χρήματα τῆς διοικήσεως, the annual surplus of regular revenue over peace-time expenses—in war time the surplus went by law to the war fund, τὰ στρατιωτικά[63]—and was used for making distributions to the citizens at the rate of 2 obols a head on some festival days.[64] According to Demosthenes even the well-to-do drew it;[65] let us then suppose that of the 21,000 citizens[66] as many as 18,000 actually took the money. The cost would then be 1 talent per day.

The number of distributions varied according to the state of the fund. One lexicographer mentions a drachma as the total in 395–394 B.C.;[67] that is three distributions were made, probably for the three days of the Dionysia. Another lexicographer speaks of payments for the Dionysia and the Panathenaea[68]—six days in all. Hypereides[69] mentions a man who impersonated his son who was abroad, and was fined a talent for the sake of 5 drachmae; this sum he may well have drawn over several years. But assuming that 5 drachmae represents a year's takings, that is that distributions were made on as many as fifteen days, the annual expenditure would be 15 talents, or one-quarter of a 1 per cent εἰσφορά.

The only evidence that large sums were involved is an anecdote in Plutarch,[70] that when the Athenians were eager to launch a fleet to assist the rebels against Alexander, Demades quenched their ardour by stating that the money would have to come from a sum which he had reserved for a distribution at the rate of 50 drachmae a head for the feast of the Choes. If this anecdote has any historical basis, I am inclined to link it with another, according to which Lycurgus (very uncharacteristically) distributed the confiscated estate of one Diphilus to the people at the rate of 50 drachmae (or some say 1 mina) a head.[71] The incident will presumably have taken place in 331, when King Agis was taking the field, and Demades and Lycurgus seem to have been working together to keep Athens out of the war. This payment of 50 drachmae was then not a normal theoric distribution, but a special bonus, arising from a windfall to the treasury.

Be that as it may, all the evidence shows that in the middle of the fourth century the θεωρικόν must have been financially very small beer, and Demosthenes was rather foolish to make himself and his policy unpopular by trying to transfer it to the war fund even in peace time. When the revenue was as low as 130 talents a year, it was no doubt irritating to see even half a dozen talents squandered, and Demosthenes fell into Eubulus' trap. Later, when the revenue had risen to 400 talents, he changed his mind, and in the *Fourth Philippic* he argues— somewhat sophistically—in favour of the θεωρικόν.[72]

Politically the θεωρικόν was, as Demades put it, ἡ κόλλα τῆς δημοκρατίας, the glue of the democracy,[73] because all classes found it useful. The poor, which would include not only the thetes but a substantial proportion of the hoplites, naturally found even so tiny a dole very acceptable, since it enabled them to enjoy their festivals with a clear conscience. To the rich it was a valuable political weapon for the policy of peace or appeasement which they favoured. Eubulus could threaten not only εἰσφοραί, which affected only 6000 voters, but the transfer of the θεωρικόν to the war fund, which affected all the citizens, if the assembly would not vote for the Peace of Philocrates.[74] Meidias could say, 'Do you expect me to pay war tax for you while you receive distributions?'[75] A large part of the *Fourth Philippic* is devoted to combating the argument of the well-to-do citizens that they cannot be expected to pay war tax and perform trierarchies if the poor draw their dole.[76]

It is somewhat paradoxical that the leaders of the peace party should have been a group of the very wealthy men who, owing to the inefficiency of the Athenian financial machine, contributed least in proportion to their means to war expenses. But, this being so, this very inefficiency played into their hands, for war inflicted disproportionate hardship on every other class. Even the well-to-do, the less wealthy of the 1200 members of the trierarchic symmories, bore an unfair proportion of naval expenses. The more modest war taxpayers were hard pressed to pay their share of the levy. The humble hoplites and the thetes looked forward with dread to being called up for prolonged unpaid foreign service in the army and the fleet, and moreover had to sacrifice their theoric doles. It was these last who really suffered the most by war, yet it was they who, if roused to action, voted for war. On Alexander's death, Diodorus[77] tells us, the men of property (οἱ κτηματικοί) urged that Athens stay quiet, and it was the masses (τὰ πλήθη) who responded to the appeals of the orators of the war party, and declared the Lamian war, in which Athens played so prominent and so creditable a part.

It is understandable that the masses should have required some rousing to vote for war, when it meant such hardship for them. What is less easy to understand is why, once involved in war, they did not vote levies of tax which would have provided them with adequate pay for hoplite and naval service. The war taxpayers numbered only about 6000, well under a third of the total citizen body of 21,000, and one might have expected the majority of the assembly to vote eagerly for a tax which they would not have to pay. In this connexion it is worth noting the language that Demosthenes uses. He never urges the poor to soak the rich; on the contrary he appeals to the assembly to pay tax themselves. In every passage save one the war taxpayers are alluded to in the second person,[78] and the one exception is significant. It is in the speech on the symmories, where Demosthenes is curbing a warlike assembly and deprecating a levy; here he says, 'Suppose *you* want *us* to pay a 12½ per cent tax?'[79] The inference seems to be that, contrary to general belief, the average assembly was attended mainly by the relatively well-to-do citizens, so that the war tax-payers were, if not in a majority, a substantial part of the audience, and that it was only at moments of crisis—the speech on the symmories was delivered to combat a war scare that the Persian king was about to attack Athens—that the poorer classes came in force and might outvote those who would have to pay the tax.

If this was so in the assembly, it was even more markedly so in the law courts, where so many political issues were ultimately decided by way of the γραφὴ παρανόμων. We generally picture the law courts as manned by the very poor, eager to earn their 3 obols, but the language of Demosthenes and his contemporaries is hardly consistent with this view. The *Meidias*, with its constant appeal to prejudice against wealth, might seem at first sight to support it. But Meidias is represented as very rich, and moreover ostentatious, a bully and a shirker of his public obligations, and it is noteworthy that Demosthenes finds it necessary to apologize for introducing a really poor witness, the arbitrator Strato, who is a hoplite.[80] The speech might well have been delivered to a well-to-do audience of οἱ εὔποροι or οἱ τὰς οὐσίας ἔχοντες (phrases of commendation in other speeches), who would probably dislike an insolent πλούσιος (consistently a term of abuse) more than would the very poor. In the *Androtion* and the *Timocrates* Demosthenes depicts the woes of the humbler payers of war tax in a way which he evidently expects to excite the sympathy of his audience—a really poor audience would not have felt very indignant at Androtion's distraining his victims' single maidservants when they had none themselves.[81] The *Leptines* is a very strange speech to deliver to a poor audience. Not a word is said about the effect of the law on the masses, in their capacity of either audiences to the spectacles produced by the choregi or of dancers in the choruses.[82] Leptines' plea was that his law would relieve the (comparatively) poor from the burden of liturgies by abolishing the exemptions of the rich, and Demosthenes tries to prove that the quashing of the law will not adversely affect the class who had to undertake liturgies:[83] his speech must have been addressed to a jury drawn mainly from that class. Even more revealing is a remark in Deinarchus' speech against Demosthenes,[84] where he appeals to any jurors who were members of the 300 when Demosthenes passed his trierarchic law to tell their neighbours how he was bribed to amend it. Such an appeal would have been ridiculous unless members of the 300, the richest men in Athens, frequently sat on juries.

Upon reflexion this is not unnatural. The greatest political issues and the fate of statesmen were decided in the courts. Would it not be prudent for leading politicians to get their supporters to enrol in the 6000 jurors? They were not obliged to empanel themselves every day for minor cases, but could turn out in force when a *cause célèbre* was to be tried. And there was probably little competition for enrolment as a juror; a working man could not keep a family on 3 obols a day—he could only just feed himself—and he could earn three times as much even by casual unskilled labour.[85] Why the poor did not attend assemblies, where the pay was better—a drachma or even 9 obols—is more difficult to explain. They perhaps found the intricacies of politics as run by the professionals— oἱ πολιτευόμενοι—baffling, and were frustrated by finding every decree they passed taken to the courts and quashed under the γραφὴ παρανόμων.

This analysis has, I hope, helped to explain against what heavy odds Demosthenes was battling in his great struggle for Athenian democracy, and at the same time given you a more sympathetic understanding of the Athenian people to whom he spoke.

NOTES

[1] II, 62, 7.

[2] XIV, 19, 27; cf. Philochorus, *fr*. 46 (*F. Gr. H.* III, no. 328).

[3] XXVII, 9.

[4] Pollux, VIII, 130.

[5] *IG²*, II–III, 2496. Isaeus, XI, 42, assumes 8 per cent as a normal rent for land.

[6] E.g. Lysias, III, 24; Isaeus, VII, 39, XI, 47; Isocrates, VII, 35; Dem. XXVII, 8, XXVIII, 3–4, XLII, 22–3, XLV, 66; Aeschines, I, 101; cf. Plato, *Rep.* 343 D.

[7] XXVII, 7, 9, XXVIII, 4, XXIX, 59.

[8] XXVII, 37.

[9] In his new edition of Bury's *History of Greece*, p. 890.

[10] E.g. Lysias, XIX, 28–30, 42–3.

[11] Dem. XXVIII, 4, cf. XXI, 157.

[12] See note 24.

[13] Dem. XXII, 44.

[14] Leptines ἐκ Κοίλης and Callicrates son of Eupherus, whom Demosthenes cites in XXII, 60, were trierarchs (*IG²*, II–III, 1609 II, l. 72; cf. 1622 C, ll. 361–3, 375–7, and 1622 B, ll. 165–6).

[15] Dem. XXII, 60. I have assumed that this paragraph refers to the arrears which Androtion actually collected, seven talents according to XXII, 44. If the whole fourteen talents were in small sums the total of debtors would be about double.

[16] Isaeus, VI, 60 καὶ τὰς εἰσφορὰς εἰσενηνόχασιν ἀμφότεροι πάσας ἐν τοῖς τριακοσίοις . . . εἰς δὲ τοὺς τριακοσίους ἐγγέγραπται καὶ εἰσφέρει τὰς εἰσφοράς.

[17] Cf. the incident recorded in Dem. III, 4–5.

[18] Dem. L, 8.

[19] See note 16.

[20]   Dem. L, 9 shows that προεισφορά was a liturgy subject to the normal rules.

[21]   This is implied by Dem. L, 8–9 προσεπηνέχθη μου τοὔνομα ἐν τριττοῖς δήμοις...τούτων ἐγώ...ἔθηκα τὰς προεισφορὰς πρῶτος.

[22]   Dem. L, 10.

[23]   XXIV, 111; cf. I, 20, II, 31, where, addressing the assembly, he speaks loosely of everyone paying εἰσφορά.

[24]   The evidence is Cleidemus (fr. 8, F. Gr. H. III, no. 323) quoted by Photius, s.v. ναυκραρία: he speaks of 100 symmories, and these must be those of the εἰσφορά, since the trierarchic symmories numbered only 20 (Dem. XIV, 17). The figure is confirmed by the 300 προεισφέροντες (Dem. XLII, 25); for the 300 seem to be identical with τοὺς ἡγεμόνας τῶν συμμοριῶν ἢ τοὺς δευτέρους καὶ τρίτους (Dem. XVIII, 103; cf. Aeschines, c. Ctes. 222). We know from Dem. XXVIII, 4, XXI, 157 that the εἰσφορά symmories had ἡγεμόνες whereas the trierarchic had ἐπιμεληταί (Dem. XLVII, 21, 22, 24).

[25]   Dem. XIV, 16–7.   [26]   XXVII, 7, XXVIII, 4.

[27]   XXIX, 59.   [28]   Diodorus, XVIII, 18, 4–5.

[29]   XXII, 44.   [30]   XXVII, 37.

[31]   Xenophon, Hell. VI, ii, 1.

[32]   XIV, 27; cf. III, 4 for a war tax of sixty talents (1 per cent) actually voted if not collected.

[33]   XXII, 65 (=XXIV, 172) οἱ γεωργοῦντες καὶ φειδόμενοι διὰ παιδοτροφίας δὲ καὶ οἰκεῖα ἀναλώματα καὶ λειτουργίας ἑτέρας ἐκλελοιπότες εἰσφοράς. This is not to say that all who owed arrears of εἰσφορά were poor men. Cf. note 14.

[34]   Dem. XLII, 22.

[35]   Lysias, XIX, 29, 42. Aristophanes bought more than 300 plethra of land and a house (of the value of 50 minae) for rather more than 5 talents. The price works out at about 85 drachmae the plethron, or about 360 drachmae the acre.

[36]   Cf. note 5.   [37]   Cf. note 45.

[38] xv, 107–13.   [39]   Dem. xlix, 6–21.

[40] Xenophon, *Hell.* vi, ii, 37.

[41] *Ibid.* vi, v, 49; Diodorus, xv, 84, 2, xvi, 37, 3; 85, 2, xviii, 10, 2; 11, 3.

[42] iv, 21.   [43]   iv, 28–9.

[44] Aristotle, 'Αθ. Πολ. 42, 3.

[45] The Eleusis accounts of 329 B.C. (*IG²*, ii–iii, 1672, ll. 4–5, 42–3, 117–18, 141–2).

[46] xix, 84 ἡ πρότερον βοήθει' εἰς Πύλας... ἥν μετὰ πλειόνων ἢ διακοσίων ταλάντων ἐποιήσασθε, ἂν λογίσησθε τὰς ἰδίας δαπάνας τὰς τῶν στρατευσαμένων.

[47] ι, 27 εἰ γὰρ ὑμᾶς δεήσειεν αὐτοὺς τριάκονθ' ἡμέρας μόνας ἔξω γενέσθαι, καὶ ὅσ' ἀνάγκη στρατοπέδῳ χρωμένους τῶν ἐκ τῆς χώρας λαμβάνειν, μηδενὸς ὄντος ἐν αὐτῇ πολεμίου λέγω, πλείον' ἂν οἶμαι ζημιωθῆναι τοὺς γεωργοῦντας ὑμῶν ἢ ὅσ' εἰς ἅπαντα τὸν πρὸ τοῦ πόλεμον δεδαπάνησθε.

[48] Thucydides, iii, 17, 4.

[49] It appears from Harpocration, *s.v.* θῆτες (citing Aristophanes), that θῆτες did not serve as hoplites; cf. Thuc. iii, 16, 1, vi, 43, viii, 24, 2. The Solonian classes were by the fourth century based on property, not income (Isaeus, vii, 39). The figure of 2000 drachmae for zeugites is an inference from Diodorus, xviii, 18, 4–5, on the assumption that Antipater set up a hoplite franchise. The figure was probably reached by multiplying by ten the Solonian income of 200 μέτρα (Arist. 'Αθ. Πολ. 7, 4), converted on the Solonian scale of values (Plut. *Solon*, 23) into 200 drachmae: this figure is slightly confirmed by the value of the Lesbian κλῆροι (Thuc. iii, 50, 2) which were probably intended to raise thetic occupants to zeugite status.

[50] xxi, 83, 95.   [51]   Lysias, xvi, 14.

[52] Isocrates, viii, 48; Dem. xxi, 154–5 (cf. L, 6–7, 16, iii, 4, iv, 36).

[53] That this was the rate till the Sicilian disaster (when it was halved, Thuc. viii, 45, 3) is shown by Thuc. iii, 17, 4, vi, 31, 3; cf. vi, 8, 1 (a trireme costs a talent a month).

27

[54] Dem. L, 10, 12, 14, 23, 53.

[55] *Ibid.* 11–12. [56] XLIX, 11–12.

[57] L, 17, 56. [58] XLVII, 21, 44.

[59] XXI, 154–5, XVIII, 102–4.

[60] XIV, 16–20. It should be observed that the trierarchic symmories are under this scheme to provide σώματα (persons to act as trierarchs), but that the expense is to fall on the whole τίμημα τῆς χώρας of 6000 talents.

[61] Dem. XVIII, 102–4; Aeschines, *c. Ctes.* 222; Harpocration, *s.v.* συμμορία (citing Hypereides).

[62] Dem. XIII, 2 τἀργύριον μέν ἐστι τοῦθ', ὑπὲρ οὗ βουλεύ-εσθε, μικρόν, τὸ δ' ἔθος μέγα, ὃ γίγνεται μετὰ τούτου.

[63] LIX, 4–5; for the meaning of διοίκησις see XXIV, 96–101.

[64] I, 19–20, XIII, 2, 10; cf. III, 10–13, 19, 31, Harpocration, *s.v.* θεωρικά, Suidas, *s.v.* θεωρικά, θεωρικόν, Libanius, *Hypoth. in Olynth.* I, 4.

[65] X, 38.

[66] I accept Plutarch, *Phocion* 28, 7, as against Diodorus, XVIII, 18, 5, because Plutarch's figure of 12,000 thetes, added to Diodorus' 9000 hoplites, produces a total of 21,000 which tallies with (*a*) the census of Demetrius of Phalerum (Athenaeus, VI, 272C), which gave 21,000 citizens; (*b*) Dem. XXV, 50 (20,000 citizens, which is not a conventional figure like the μύριοι of XXII, 35); (*c*) Dem. III, 4 (a call-up of the twenty to forty-five age groups of θῆτες to man forty ships, i.e. to provide 8000 men); (*d*) [Plutarch], *Vit. X Or., Lycurgus, Mor.*, 843D (the confiscated property of Diphilus, worth 160 talents, was distributed between the citizens at 50, or as others say, 100 drachmae each—yielding the result of 19,000 + on the 50 drachmae basis).

[67] Hesychius, *s.v.* δραχμὴ χαλαζῶσα; cf. Harpocration, *s.v.* θεωρικά.

[68] Hesychius, *s.v.* θεωρικὰ χρήματα.

[69] I, xxvi (ed. Blass). [70] *Mor.* 818 E F.

28

[71] [Plut.], *Vitae X Or.*, *Lycurgus* (*Mor.* 843 D).

[72] Dem. X, 35–43. [73] Plut. *Mor.* 1011 B.

[74] Dem. XIX, 291. [75] Dem. XXI, 203.

[76] X, 35 ff., esp. 39.

[77] XVIII, 10, cf. *Hell. Oxy.* 1, 3, and Aristophanes, *Eccl.* 197–8, for a similar situation in the early fourth century.

[78] E.g. I, 6, 20, II, 24, 27, 31, III, 33, IV, 7, VIII, 23, X, 19.

[79] XIV, 27.

[80] XXI, 83, 95. Cf. the very apologetic and humble tone taken to the jury by a really poor litigant in LVII, esp. 25, 31, 35, 45.

[81] XXII, 47 ff., XXIV, 160 ff., esp. 197.

[82] He merely says airily that there will always be enough men to perform the liturgies (XX, 22), a statement refuted by XXI, 13. [Xen.] 'Aθ. Πολ. I, 13, emphasizes how the δῆμος draws money from the choregi and gymnasiarchs ᾄδων καὶ τρέχων καὶ ὀρχούμενος.

[83] Leptines' law opened with the preamble ὅπως ἂν οἱ πλουσιώτατοι λητουργῶσιν (XX, 127), and his argument, which Demosthenes tries to refute, was ὡς αἱ λειτουργίαι νῦν μὲν εἰς πένητας ἀνθρώπους ἔρχονται, ἐκ δὲ τοῦ νόμου τούτου λητουργήσουσιν οἱ πλουσιώτατοι (XX, 18).

[84] Deinarchus, *in Dem.* 42.

[85] In the Eleusinian accounts (*IG*², II–III, 1672) of 329 B.C., 3 obols is allowed for τροφή for the public slaves (ll. 4–5, 42–3, 117–18, 141–2); casual labourers (μισθωτοί) doing unskilled work get 1½ drachmae (ll. 28–30, 32–4, 45–6, 60–2); skilled men get 2 drachmae (ll. 110–11, carpenters, 177–8, stone polishers) or 2½ drachmae (26–8, bricklayers, 31–2, stone masons).

29

This inaugural lecture, delivered in Cambridge on 23 January 1952 by A. H. M. Jones, Professor of Ancient History in the University of Cambridge, was published in 1952 by the Syndics of the Cambridge University Press, and printed in Great Britain at the University Press, Cambridge (Brooke Crutchley, University Printer).

www.ingramcontent.com/pod-product-compliance
Ingram Content Group UK Ltd.
Pitfield, Milton Keynes, MK11 3LW, UK
UKHW020449010325
455719UK00015B/493